W9-AYU-800

LANGUAGE LOGIC TWISTERS

RUN-ON RIDDLERS

Level A Book 1

M.A. Hockett

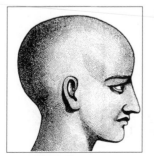

© 2002

CRITICAL THINKING BOOKS & SOFTWARE

www.CriticalThinking.com

P.O. Box 448 • Pacific Grove • CA 93950-0448

Phone 800-458-4849 • FAX 831-393-3277

ISBN 0-89455-817-X

Printed in the United States of America

To Bob ,

Thanks for your patience.

Edited by Cheryl Block

The images used herein were obtained from IMSI's MasterClips® Premium Image Collection, 1895 Francisco Blvd. East, San Rafael, CA 94901-5506, USA.

TABLE OF CONTENTS

INTRODUCTION

The English language is rife with possibilities. The same words that create one meaning by themselves, or with other words, can create an entirely different meaning when attached to the next sentence. Much confusion (as well as amusement) can result if we fail to separate our intended meanings.

Run-on Riddlers gives practice in using context clues to correct run-ons and fragments. The activities are based on the idea that punctuation and capitals are necessary to make written communication clear. Students have to read and follow directions carefully—and they must really *think,* using context clues for analyzing, comparing, contrasting, and deducing. Students must then determine where to place capitals and ending punctuation so that the sentences communicate the intended meaning.

Run-on Riddlers may be used for specific practice with run-ons and fragments in context or as part of a systematic program for developing language mechanics and thinking skills. Each page includes instructions and can be used for independent practice. For students requiring instruction or remediation in grammar rules, you may also want to use *The Language Mechanic,* available from Critical Thinking Books & Software. For more practice applying grammar and punctuation rules in context, you may want to use *Editor in Chief.*®

Run-on Riddlers' activity content is uniquely designed to facilitate the use of deductive reasoning in conjunction with run-on and fragmented sentences. It presents examples which portray distinct differences in meaning based on where a run-on is divided. For example, notice the difference in meaning of the same words when you change only the punctuation and capitalization:

> *The ice cream was white, and black dogs lapped it up.*

> *The ice cream was white and black. Dogs lapped it up.*

Run-on Riddlers uses this concept to advantage. Students must use context clues that are sometimes embedded as information in the same sentence or in an adjacent sentence, or as pictures.

Some activities require only editing, others require rewriting; the final section includes a writing challenge in which students may use pictures as the stimuli for creating their own "two-way" phrases and sentences.

For some students, it will be a new idea to look for subtle differences in context in order to decide how to punctuate. For those who need further guidance, see the Sample Lessons on p. 34.

Warmup: Before and After

Directions: Each line can be made into two sentences if a word or phrase is repeated. Underline the words that should repeat to make two complete sentences. Rewrite the sentences, adding capitals and periods as needed.

Example: The goose laid <u>one egg</u> is all I need for breakfast.

The goose laid one egg. One egg is all I need for breakfast.

1.   **She looked like a monkey business is sneaky.**

   _____

   _____

2.   **London Bridge is falling down hurts your knees.**

   _____

   _____

3.   **Peter Piper led the children followed him like rats.**

   _____

   _____

4.   **I'll love you forever has more days than I can count.**

   _____

   _____

RULE: A sentence has at least one subject and one verb. It begins with a capital and ends with a period, question mark, or exclamation mark. It clearly shows at least one idea.

Warmup: Before and After

Directions: Each line can be made into two sentences if a word or phrase is repeated. Underline the words that should repeat to make two complete sentences. Rewrite the sentences, adding capitals and periods as needed.

Example: The goose laid <u>one egg</u> is all I need for breakfast.

The goose laid one egg. One egg is all I need for breakfast.

5.   **Spaghetti is slippery food makes you slide on the floor.**

_____

_____

6.   **The Great Squash rises from the garden party was fun.**

_____

_____

7.   **Don't sit on a porcupine has very sharp quills!**

_____

_____

8.   **He rode his skateboard parks are becoming popular.**

_____

_____

9.   **You barked up the wrong tree is never the right tree.**

_____

_____

RULE: A sentence has at least one subject and one verb. It begins with a capital and ends with a period, question mark, or exclamation mark. It clearly shows at least one idea.

Over Easy

Directions: Read the directions for each activity. Create complete sentences that make sense with the rest of the text. • To add a capital, cross out a lowercase letter and write the capital letter above it. • Cross out any unnecessary capitals and periods. • Add ending punctuation where it belongs.

EXAMPLE

The line below is correct as is.

I always eat eggs. At eight o'clock, I go to school.

Correct the line below to make two sentences. (The picture shows what happens at the table.) Cross out a capital and a period. Add a capital and a period.

We always eat eggs. At the table we go to school later.

ANSWER:

We always eat eggs~~.~~ ~~A~~t the table. ^W^~~w~~e go to school later.

EXPLANATION: We can tell from the picture that *at the table* goes with the first sentence. *At the table we go to school later* would not make sense.

Now try it yourself.

1. The first line below is correct as it is. Correct the second line. Cross out a lowercase letter and write a capital above it. Add a period and a question mark.

    I ate. The hotcakes were all I could hold.

    I ate the hotcakes were all of them yours

RULE: A sentence has at least one subject and one verb. It begins with a capital and ends with a period, question mark, or exclamation mark. It clearly shows at least one idea. It may contain two ideas separated by a conjunction.

Over Easy

Directions: Create complete sentences. • To add a capital, cross out a lowercase letter and write the capital letter above it. • Cross out any unnecessary capitals and periods. • Add ending punctuation where it belongs.

2. Use the picture below to decide the meaning of the text. Add a period and a capital to correct it.

    They are small dark monsters frighten them.

3. The first line is correct. Show a different meaning for the second line by adding a capital and a period.

    They drive fast cars. Zoom down the road.

    They drive fast cars zoom down the road.

4. Find the meanings of *a* and *b* below. Capitalize and add ending punctuation (periods or exclamation mark) to correct each.

    a. **We're out on the jungle gym help us we are falling**

    b. **We're out in the jungle Jim will help us he can reach high**

RULE: A sentence has at least one subject and one verb. It begins with a capital and ends with a period, question mark, or exclamation mark. It clearly shows at least one idea. It may contain two ideas separated by a conjunction.

Over Easy

Directions: Create complete sentences. • To add a capital, cross out a lowercase letter and write the capital letter above it. • Cross out any unnecessary capitals and periods. • Add ending punctuation where it belongs.

5. Which picture shows what the cat does? Add two capitals and two periods to make three sentences.

   The cat rolls the ball bounces the mouse runs away.

6. The picture below shows the wrong meaning. Create three sentences. Add two capitals and two periods.

   The repairman is at the door let him in the dryer needs fixing.

7. Find the meaning below. Capitalize and add ending punctuation to make three correct sentences.

   Tie your shoe string those beads we will be ready to go.

RULE: A sentence has at least one subject and one verb. It begins with a capital and ends with a period, question mark, or exclamation mark. It clearly shows at least one idea. It may contain two ideas separated by a conjunction.

Over Easy

Directions: Create complete sentences. • To add a capital, cross out a lowercase letter and write the capital letter above it. • Cross out any unnecessary capitals and periods. • Add ending punctuation where it belongs.

8.   Which picture shows the meaning? Add a period, a capital, and a question mark to make two sentences.

   She felt the hot sun was moving the snowman going to save him

9.   Figure out what the sentences mean. Each line should be two sentences. Capitalize and add ending punctuation to correct the sentences.

   a.   **We shouldn't run the red light is blinking**

   b.   **We shouldn't run the red light is it blinking**

10.   Find the meanings below. Capitalize and add ending punctuation.

   a.   **I will go when he wants me**

   b.   **I will go when does he want me**

RULE: A sentence has at least one subject and one verb. It begins with a capital and ends with a period, question mark, or exclamation mark. It clearly shows at least one idea. It may contain two ideas separated by a conjunction.

Over Easy

Directions: Create complete sentences. • To add a capital, cross out a lowercase letter and write the capital letter above it. • Cross out any unnecessary capitals and periods. • Add ending punctuation where it belongs.

11. The picture goes with the text. Add two ending punctuation marks and a capital to make two sentences.

   She irons her hair isn't straight hair in style

12. The sentences below are separated in the wrong place. Cross out a period and a capital and write a period and capital where they make sense.

   He walked in the door to the house of mirrors.
   Slammed shut.

13. Find the meaning of the run-on sentence below. Add a period and a capital to correct it.

   She stumbled around in the dark morning would be brighter.

> **RULE:** A sentence has at least one subject and one verb. It begins with a capital and ends with a period, question mark, or exclamation mark. It clearly shows at least one idea. It may contain two ideas separated by a conjunction.

Over Easy

Directions: Create complete sentences. • To add a capital, cross out a lowercase letter and write the capital letter above it. • Cross out any unnecessary capitals and periods. • Add ending punctuation where it belongs.

14. Which picture shows the meaning? Add a period and a capital to make two sentences.

Bob has trouble seeing the giraffe wearing those glasses makes it easy for the giraffe to see Bob, though!

15. Find the meanings below. Add capitals and ending punctuation to correct the sentences.

   a. **I always drive in the house is where I find my keys**

   b. **He always drives in the house with his toy truck**

16. Find the meanings below. Add capitals and ending punctuation to correct the sentences.

   a. **The children run into the tree see the squirrels jump**

   b. **The children run into the tree go the squirrels**

RULE: A sentence has at least one subject and one verb. It begins with a capital and ends with a period, question mark, or exclamation mark. It clearly shows at least one idea. It may contain two ideas separated by a conjunction.

Over Easy

Directions: Create complete sentences. • To add a capital, cross out a lowercase letter and write the capital letter above it. • Cross out any unnecessary capitals and periods. • Add ending punctuation where it belongs.

17. Find the meanings below. Capitalize and add ending punctuation to correct the sentences.

They speak Spanish rice is their choice for dinner they don't like Spanish rice, though

We are French fried potatoes are our favorite food we are from France, and we have never been fried

18. Find the meanings below. Capitalize and add ending punctuation to correct the sentences.

You lost your skate board the plane without it

You lost your skateboard the plane will leave any minute

19. Find the meaning below. Capitalize and add ending punctuation to correct the sentence.

She swatted the fly having two-foot arms made it easy

> **RULE:** A sentence has at least one subject and one verb. It begins with a capital and ends with a period, question mark, or exclamation mark. It clearly shows at least one idea. It may contain two ideas separated by a conjunction.

Over Easy

Directions: Create complete sentences. • To add a capital, cross out a lowercase letter and write the capital letter above it. • Cross out any unnecessary capitals and periods. • Add ending punctuation where it belongs.

20. Use the picture to help find the meaning. Add a period and capital.

The ice cream was white and black dogs lapped it up.

21. Find the meaning below. Add one capital and one period to make two sentences.

The ground is hard and dry rain soaks into it.

22. Find the meanings below. Capitalize and add ending punctuation to make four sentences altogether.

Watch your foot ball playing is fun if you're careful

Watch your football playing is fun, but you might lose your ball

23. Find the meanings below. Capitalize and add ending punctuation to correct the sentences.

They are ready to celebrate up in the air go their hats

We are ready to celebrate up in the air get in the balloon

RULE: A sentence has at least one subject and one verb. It begins with a capital and ends with a period, question mark, or exclamation mark. It clearly shows at least one idea. It may contain two ideas separated by a conjunction.

Over Easy

Directions: Create complete sentences. • To add a capital, cross out a lowercase letter and write the capital letter above it. • Cross out any unnecessary capitals and periods. • Add ending punctuation where it belongs.

24. The picture shows the wrong meaning. Add a capital and period to show the right meaning.

    He can't eat it all at once, but he can eat a sandwich whole sandwiches must be cut into tiny pieces for him.

25. Find the meaning below. Add two capitals and two periods to make three sentences.

    The sign says there is a drawing for a free vacation we think we'll need that sign up the family.

26. Find the meaning. Correct the text by adding one capital and one period.

    I know you want to play, but we already picked our teammates sit on the bench and watch all the teammates play.

27. Add a capital and a period to make two sentences.

    We saw all the flowers lie in the field so you can see them up close.

RULE: A sentence has at least one subject and one verb. It begins with a capital and ends with a period, question mark, or exclamation mark. It clearly shows at least one idea. It may contain two ideas separated by a conjunction.

Over Easy

Directions: Create complete sentences. • To add a capital, cross out a lowercase letter and write the capital letter above it. • Cross out any unnecessary capitals and periods. • Add ending punctuation where it belongs.

28.   The example is written correctly to go with its picture.

Example: *The reptile slithered as the man was walking. The snake wasn't that unusual.*

Fix the sentences below to go with the picture below. Cross out a period and capital. Add punctuation and a capital to make a statement and a question.

The reptile slithered as the man was walking. The snake wasn't that unusual.

29.   Make two sentences by crossing out a capital and a period.

Don't drive at a high speed. Traps. Are bound to catch you.

RULE: A sentence has at least one subject and one verb. It begins with a capital and ends with a period, question mark, or exclamation mark. It clearly shows at least one idea. It may contain two ideas separated by a conjunction.

Over Easy

Directions: Create complete sentences. • To add a capital, cross out a lowercase letter and write the capital letter above it. • Cross out any unnecessary capitals and periods. • Add ending punctuation where it belongs.

30.   Are the sentences below complete? If not, cross out a period and a capital to make two sensible sentences.

That's my favorite. Color. The picture orange.

31.   Do the sentences below make sense? If not, change a period and capital so all three sentences make sense together.

The soup was good. Cold children ate it. They were too hot to eat it warm.

32.   Use context and common sense to make three sentences, adding a capital and periods.

Josh couldn't do his sewing project I made his shirt cook my dinner, and I'll make yours.

RULE: A sentence has at least one subject and one verb. It begins with a capital and ends with a period, question mark, or exclamation mark. It clearly shows at least one idea. It may contain two ideas separated by a conjunction.

Running Picks: Multiple Choice

Directions: Circle the letter of the best correction for each activity. You will see sentences that have commas. However, you will not be asked to edit for comma usage. The pictures are not clues.

1. To relax, she takes a walk at night in the sky shine many stars.

   a. To relax, she takes a walk at night. In the sky shine many stars.

   b. To relax, she takes a walk at night in the sky. Shine many stars.

2. She wrestled the pigs to keep clean she took a bath.

   a. She wrestled the pigs to keep clean. She took a bath.

   b. She wrestled the pigs. To keep clean, she took a bath.

3. He picked up bagels on his way to school he was late for class.

   a. He picked up bagels on his way to school. He was late for class.

   b. He picked up bagels. On his way to school, he was late for class.

RULE: A sentence has at least one subject and one verb. It begins with a capital and ends with a period, question mark, or exclamation mark. It clearly shows at least one idea. It may contain two ideas separated by a conjunction.

Running Picks: Multiple Choice

Directions: Circle the letter of the best correction for each activity. You will see sentences that have commas. However, you will not be asked to edit for comma usage. The pictures are not clues.

4.   He heard the teacher speak gently in his usual rough manner Charlie made fun of his knowledge

    a.   He heard the teacher speak gently in his usual rough manner. Charlie made fun of his knowledge.

    b.   He heard the teacher speak gently. In his usual rough manner, Charlie made fun of his knowledge.

    c.   He heard the teacher speak. Gently in his usual rough manner, Charlie made fun of his knowledge.

5.   He tore open the game and he scrambled to grab the stuff that fell out and collected all the little pieces

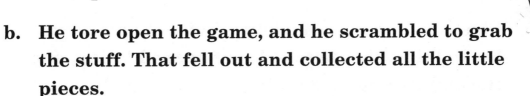

    a.   He tore open the game and he scrambled. To grab the stuff that fell out. He collected all the little pieces.

    b.   He tore open the game, and he scrambled to grab the stuff. That fell out and collected all the little pieces.

    c.   He tore open the game. He scrambled to grab the stuff that fell out, and then he collected all the little pieces.

RULE: A sentence has at least one subject and one verb. It begins with a capital and ends with a period, question mark, or exclamation mark. It clearly shows at least one idea. It may contain two ideas separated by a conjunction.

Running Picks: Multiple Choice

Directions: Circle the letter of the best correction for each paragraph. You will see sentences that have commas. However, you will not be asked to edit for comma usage. The pictures are not clues.

6. Lazily the cat Marvin sprawled on the sofa with a lively bounce Emy tossed him off

   a. **Lazily, the cat Marvin sprawled. On the sofa with a lively bounce, Emy tossed him off.**

   b. **Lazily, the cat Marvin sprawled on the sofa with a lively bounce. Emy tossed him off.**

   c. **Lazily, the cat Marvin sprawled on the sofa. With a lively bounce, Emy tossed him off.**

7. She lived in a dirt shack and her feet were blackened by walking the thatched roof needed fixing and the children needed milk

   a. **She lived in a dirt shack, and her feet were blackened by walking. The thatched roof needed fixing, and the children needed milk.**

   b. **She lived in a dirt shack her feet were blackened by. Walking, the thatched roof needed fixing, and the children needed milk.**

   c. **She lived in a dirt shack, and her feet were blackened by walking the thatched roof. Needed fixing and the children needed milk.**

RULE: A sentence has at least one subject and one verb. It begins with a capital and ends with a period, question mark, or exclamation mark. It clearly shows at least one idea. It may contain two ideas separated by a conjunction.

Running Edits

Directions: Make the number of sentences asked for. Add or cross out capital letters and punctuation where necessary. You will cross out some *ands*.

1. Four sentences

   Something was odd. About the new teacher. Mr. Sol was at the front of the room. When Hal looked down at his math book. When Hal looked up again, Mr. Sol had disappeared a cough told Hal that Mr. Sol was now looking over Hal's shoulder.

2. Five sentences: Cross out two *ands*.

   I trained my dog. To cook my breakfast and he's pretty good. At mixing pancake batter. And he can even pour it on the griddle he has trouble, though, when it comes to flipping the pancakes on his nose is where they land!

3. Four sentences: Cross out one *and*.

   We watched the farm animals get smaller and smaller floating over the countryside in a hot air balloon. Was fun. Dad turned on the burners to keep the air warm in the balloon and the reason the balloon can float above the land is that hot air is lighter than cool air.

> **RULE:** A sentence has at least one subject and one verb. It begins with a capital and ends with a period, question mark, or exclamation mark. It clearly shows at least one idea. It may contain two ideas separated by a conjunction.

Running Edits

Directions: Make the number of sentences asked for. Add or cross out capital letters and punctuation where necessary. You will cross out some *ands*.

4.   Five sentences: Cross out one *and*.

Her friend had a comfortable home. Yolanda wondered. What that would be like. Living in a real house. Should be a lot easier than living in her hut. The little shack. Was simple and small and had no electricity and it was a good thing she had a cell phone and a laptop computer.

5.   Five sentences: Cross out two *ands*.

Chocolate is made from the beans of the cacao tree. And each of its seed pods. Can produce about 50 of these white beans. They are dried. In the sun they are taken indoors and packed and finally, they are sent to the candy makers.

6.   Six sentences: Cross out one *and*.

I saw a woman getting a tattoo. On her arm. The artist put the color in her skin. By giving her little shots of ink. The woman said getting the tattoo hurt like bees stinging her arm was pretty, but the tattoo would never come off and would I ever get a real tattoo I would rather get one of those stick-on tattoos!

RULE: A sentence has at least one subject and one verb. It begins with a capital and ends with a period, question mark, or exclamation mark. It clearly shows at least one idea. It may contain two ideas separated by a conjunction.

Letters Have It

1. The words below make a complete sentence, as shown (it is about dear Manuel).

    Dear Manuel has my bat.

    Rewrite the same words in the blanks below as part of a friendly letter. They will have a different meaning. Add a comma, two capitals, and a question mark where needed.

    dear Manuel has my bat arrived

    _____

    _____

    I can't wait to try it out on your softball team!

                                                    Sincerely, _____

                                                    Peggy _____

RULE: In a letter, capitalize the greeting and only the first word of the closing. Use a comma after the greeting and after the closing. Make sure all parts work together to make sense. Separate run-on meanings with capitals and punctuation.

Letters Have It

2. a. Which example below (1 or 2) shows that you are talking *about* your aunt and uncle? _____ Correct it by adding a period.

    b. In which example are you writing *to* your aunt and uncle? _____ Rewrite the words on the lines below. Add a comma, a capital, and an exclamation mark to make the letter correct.

    1) Dear Aunt Gigi and Uncle Tony have a wonderful time on their vacation

    2) Dear Aunt Gigi and Uncle Tony have a wonderful time on your vacation

    _____

    _____

    _____

    Love, _____

    Margaret _____

RULE: In a letter, capitalize the greeting and only the first word of the closing. Use a comma after the greeting and after the closing. Make sure all parts work together to make sense. Separate run-on meanings with capitals and punctuation.

Letters Have It

3.   a.   Correct the sentences as if you are talking to Tina. Add two periods and one capital to make two sentences.

I know you feel guilty about our losing the games you think the fault is yours, but it is not always yours, Tina

    b.   Using only the words given, finish rewriting the sentences as a letter from Tina. Add two capitals and two periods.

I know you feel guilty about our losing the games you think the fault is yours, but it is not yours always, Tina

Dear Reggie,

_____

_____

_____

                                          _____

                                          _____

RULE: In a letter, capitalize the greeting and only the first word of the closing. Use a comma after the greeting and after the closing. Make sure all parts work together to make sense. Separate run-on meanings with capitals and punctuation.

Letters Have It

4. In the blanks, rewrite the words below as a friendly letter. Add
    two capitals, two commas, and a period.

    **Dear uncle Janine said you would not like the
    exchange student, but I know you will love Bjorn**

    _____

    _____

    _____

    _____

    _____

    _____

RULE: In a letter, capitalize the greeting and only the first word of the
closing. Use a comma after the greeting and after the closing. Make sure
all parts work together to make sense. Separate run-on meanings with
capitals and punctuation.

Letters Have It

5. a. Correct the text below. You are talking to Jaime about dear Billy Jo. Add the necessary capitals and periods.

Dear billy jo has a gift for you he pretends it isn't for you, but I know it is yours truly, Jaime

_____

b. Rewrite the same text as a letter to Billy *from* Jaime. Add a comma, capitals, and periods.

Dear billy jo has a gift for you he pretends it isn't for you, but I know it is yours truly, Jaime

_____

_____

_____

_____

_____

_____

RULE: In a letter, capitalize the greeting and only the first word of the closing. Use a comma after the greeting and after the closing. Make sure all parts work together to make sense. Separate run-on meanings with capitals and punctuation.

Interjections

1. Which picture goes with the meaning? Add two capitals, one period, and one exclamation mark.

    I really liked her new pet rats it just ran away.

    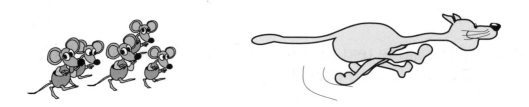

2. Find the meanings below. Add one capital, one exclamation mark, and one period.

    My great granny will not help me darn I was hoping

    she would fix the hole in my wall.

3. Find the meanings below. Add two capitals, one exclamation mark, and one period.

    I am missing the letter oh here it is. It is the letter em.

RULE: Set off an interjection as a separate exclamation. *I like eating.*
Hey! That's mine. Some common interjections are *Rats! Darn! Shoot!*
Wow! Hey! Oh!

Interjections

4. The same words can be corrected in two different ways.
    Make three sentences in *a*.

    **a. He's going for target practice with a bow and
        arrow. he wants me to go shoot I'd rather play
        soccer**

    Make three sentences and one interjection in *b*.

    **b. He's going for target practice with a bow and
        arrow. he wants me to go shoot I'd rather play
        soccer**

5. Use word spellings to help you find the meanings and correct each
    example.

    **The horses get mean if they don't eat hay give them
    that bale!**

    **The horses get mean if they don't eat hey give them
    that bale!**

RULE: Set off an interjection as a separate exclamation. *I like eating.*
Hey! That's mine. Some words used as interjections are *Rats! Darn!*
Shoot! Wow! Hey! Oh!

Quotations

1. In the sentence below, who has a spoon? _____

    "Mom is directing traffic," Veronica says, "with a spoon in her hand."

2. For each description, write the letter of the matching sentence.

    Ronik speaks loudly. ____

    Ronik wants John to play loudly. ____

    a. *Ronik says, "John, play your trumpet!" very loudly.*

    b. *Ronik says, "John, play your trumpet very loudly!"*

3. Match each sentence with the picture showing its meaning.

    "Do we get to eat that fish?" he asked with eyes wide open. ____

    "Do we have to eat that fish," he asked, "with eyes wide open?" ____

a.

b.

> **RULE:** Enclose spoken words in quotation marks.

Back and Forth Challenge

Directions: Correct each run-on with capitals and ending punctuation. Some text is repeated because it has more than one possible correction. If you think of other ways to correct them, write the corrected sentences on the lines.

1. He took a bath in the tub

   He took a bath. in the tub were lots of bubbles

   He took a bath in the tub. were lots of bubbles popping in his face

   He took a bath. in the tub were lots of bubbles popping in his face

   _____

   _____

2. The spaceships flew

   The spaceships flew around the planet

   The spaceships flew around the planet was a belt of asteroids

   The spaceships flew around the planet was a belt of asteroids acting as a shield

   The spaceships flew around the planet was a belt of asteroids acting as a shield

   _____

   _____

Back and Forth Challenge

Directions: Correct each run-on with capitals and ending punctuation. Some text is repeated because it has more than one possible correction. If you think of other ways to correct them, write the corrected sentences on the lines.

3. She picked an apple

    She picked an apple from the tree

    She picked an apple from the tree fell two

    She picked an apple from the tree fell two birds

    She picked an apple from the tree fell two birds fly away

    She picked an apple from the tree fell two birds fly away

    _____

    _____

4. A baseball was found

    A baseball was found under the window

    A baseball was found under the window were pieces of glass

    A baseball was found under the window were pieces of glass

    A baseball was found under the window were pieces of glass that fell when it crashed

    _____

    _____

Back and Forth Challenge

Directions: Correct each run-on with capitals and ending punctuation. Some text is repeated because it has more than one possible correction. If you think of other ways to correct them, write the corrected sentences on the lines.

5.   He loved to travel

     He loved to travel in Mexico

     He loved to travel in Mexico were his sisters

     He loved to travel in Mexico were his sisters working

     He loved to travel in Mexico were his sisters working on the family business

     He loved to travel in Mexico were his sisters working on the family business

     He loved to travel in Mexico were his sisters working on the family business was fun.

     He loved to travel in Mexico were his sisters working on the family business was fun.

     _____

     _____

     _____

Picture This: Creative Writing Challenge

Directions: Write a description for each picture. You may write two descriptions for the same picture and have a partner pick the correct meaning. You may draw other pictures in the space given and have a partner pick the one that shows the meaning of your sentence(s).

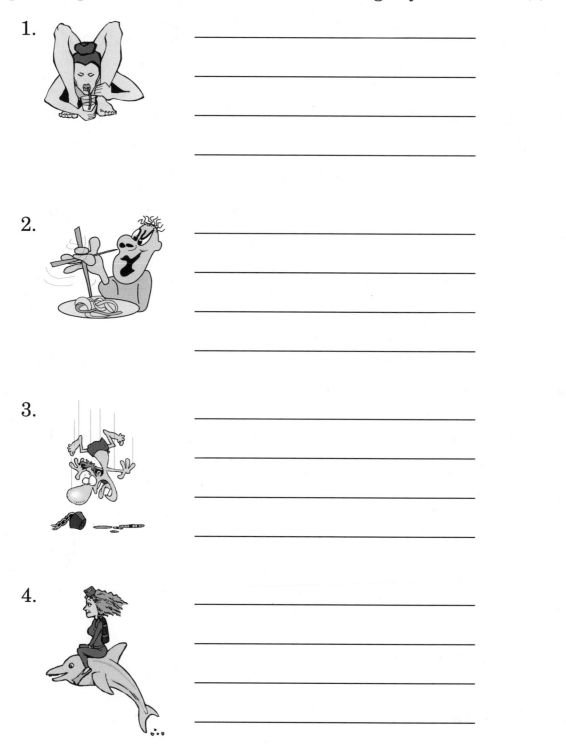

1. _____

_____

_____

_____

2. _____

_____

_____

_____

3. _____

_____

_____

_____

4. _____

_____

_____

_____

Picture This: Creative Writing Challenge

Directions: Write a description for each picture. You may write two descriptions for the same picture and have a partner pick the correct meaning. You may draw other pictures in the space given and have a partner pick the one that shows the meaning of your sentence(s).

5. _____

_____

_____

_____

6. _____

_____

_____

_____

7. _____

_____

_____

_____

8. _____

_____

_____

_____

Picture This: Creative Illustration Challenge

Directions: Have fun with the text. Draw pictures to show the intended meaning and a run-on (wrong) meaning. Have a partner correct the text and choose the picture that matches the meaning.

1.   **They are good hot dogs eat them cold or hot.**

2.   **The popsicle split the cat jumped when it slid under her belly.**

3.   **She called the man to help a large ape was following her!**

4.   **He took off his nose followed the smell and led him to dinner.**

Picture This: Creative Illustration Challenge

Directions: Have fun with the text. Draw pictures to show the intended meaning and a run-on (wrong) meaning. Have a partner correct the text and choose the picture that matches the meaning.

5. **The signs are dull yellow streetlights make them glow.**

6. **The dogs play the drums hurt their ears.**

7. **My sister runs the trains get in her way.**

8. **The horses jump the moon glows in the night.**

SAMPLE LESSONS

Some readers may already be good at picking up context clues that result in unexpected meanings. Others may need warm-up lessons to help them tune in to the "twists and turns" they may miss.

This section includes sample lessons on how to do the thinking required in each activity section. (See Table of Contents, page iii.)

Start each lesson by reviewing the importance of preventing run-on and fragmented thoughts, using the rule below.

RULE: A sentence has at least one subject and one verb. It begins with a capital and ends with a period, question mark, or exclamation mark. It clearly shows at least one idea. It may contain two ideas separated by a conjunction.

In the lessons, **T** = teacher dialog or actions and **S** = student response.

Warmup: Before and After (pp. 1–2)

T: "The different sections of the *Run-on Riddlers* will help you practice finding and fixing run-on and fragmented meanings in sentences, friendly letters. quotations, and so on. This first section is like a game to get you warmed up. It uses the idea that the very same words can end one sentence and begin another. (This game is similar to one on a popular TV show—but you don't have to guess what the letters are!)"

Show these words where all can see:
The goose laid one egg is all I need for breakfast.

T: "Here's how it works. Look at the words I've written. Your job is to make two sensible sentences. Find one word, or several words together, that could end the first sentence and begin the next sentence. Does anyone have an idea?"

[Take any student response and insert the given words twice as you read the sentences to see if they make sense.]

S: I think it's *"laid one."*

T: "Let's try it."
The goose laid one. Laid one egg is all I need for breakfast.
"Do you think it works now?"

S: "No, it doesn't make sense for the second sentence."

T: "Remember, all the words you choose must be used over again to begin the second sentence."

S: "I know—it's the words *one egg.*"

T: "Let's see what that sounds like. *The goose laid one egg. One egg is all I need for breakfast.* Does that make sense?"

S: "Yes!"

T: "Okay, you're getting the hang of it." If needed: "Let's try another."

Show these words:
London Bridge is falling down hurts your knees.

Continue in the same way as before until students come up with this:
London Bridge is falling down. Falling down hurts your knees

Note that *is falling down* doesn't work because *Is falling down hurts your knees?* has the wrong verb form (*hurts* instead of *hurting*).

T: "Okay! You're ready to do some more warmups on your own." [Pass out one or more activities from section 'Warmup: Before and After.']
"Underline the exact words that can be used to form two sensible sentences."

Additionally, if desired:
"Then, rewrite each of the two sentences, using the words you identified at the beginning of one sentence and at the end of the other."

Over Easy (pp. 3–13)

Show these words so all students can see:
They are scary dogs chase them away.

T: "Today you will practice using what you know about writing and correcting sentences to avoid run-on and fragmented meanings. First I'm going to read the words you see here. They are missing a period and capital." [Read the words with even pacing so it is unclear to which part *dogs* belongs.] "Now, can anyone tell me what is wrong with the sentence as written?"

S: "It's run together. We can't tell whether the dogs are the scary ones or the dogs are chasing the scary things."

T: "Okay. We need more to go on. What if I add this clue: *Those dogs are good watchdogs!* Now what can you tell?"

S: "Something else is scary."

T: "So what are the two sentences, and how do we show them clearly?"

S: *"They are scary. Dogs chase them away.* Put a period after *scary* and capitalize *dogs*."

T: "Good. Now, let's say the clue is a different clue: *I don't like those dogs around me!* In this case, what are the sentences?"

S: *"They are scary dogs. Chase them away!"*

T: "Right."

T: "In these activities, you will use thinking exercises to decide where to separate ideas into clear sentences. You must read directions for each activity then be detectives to find clues in the text or picture. Sometimes you will choose the picture that shows the meaning based on clues in the sentences. Then you add capitals and ending punctuation. Sometimes you will match sentences to the correct pictures. Sometimes you must decide how to divide sentences by just reading the sentences themselves."

Running Picks: Multiple Choice (pp. 14–16)

Have the example and choices below copied onto a transparency you can show on an overhead; or write it ahead of time on the blackboard; or make enlarged copies for students.

T: "In the 'Running' section of the *Run-on Riddlers*, you will read longer run-on sentences and paragraphs. You must figure out the meaning and decide which thoughts go together. From a group of choices, you must pick the best way to rewrite the sentences. I'll read a sample."

If you use an overhead, show and read aloud the run-on sentence; reveal the choices one at a time as needed.

I was so sure I could pop it that I bet my friends and I closed one eye and stuck out my tongue and I threw the dart straight and hard right into the yellow balloon.

T: "As we look at possible corrections, think about what is probably going on."
a) *I was so sure I could pop it that I bet my friends. I closed one eye, and stuck out my tongue and I threw the dart. Straight and hard right, into the yellow balloon.*

T: "Do you think this is a good correction?"

S: "No. The last sentence isn't complete."

T: "Okay, let's look at choice *b*." [Read:]
b) *I was so sure I could pop it that I bet. My friends and I closed one eye and stuck out my tongue. I threw the dart straight and hard right into the yellow balloon.*

T: "Okay, are these sentences complete? Does the choice work? Why or why not?"

S: "The sentences are complete, but it doesn't work. Your friends couldn't stick out *your* tongue."

T: "Okay, let's try another." [Read:]
c) *I was so sure I could pop it that I bet my friends. I closed one eye and stuck out my tongue. I threw the dart straight and hard right into the yellow balloon.*

T: "Does this one have complete sentences? Do they make sense together?"

S: "Yes."

T: "Good. I'm going to circle choice *c* to show it's the best choice. Now try to pick the best choices on your own."

Running Edits (pp. 17–18)

[Do the 'Running Picks' lesson as the first part of this section.]

T: "In this section, you will edit paragraphs of four to six sentences. For each you are given the number of sentences you should end up with. Here is how to make changes:
1) To join two fragments, cross out incorrect capitals and ending punctuation.
2) To separate run-on sentences, cross out the lowercase letter that should be a capital and write the capital letter above the word. Cross out the word *and* if necessary. (You are told if and how many *ands* to cross out.)"

Letters Have It (pp. 19–23)

Note: Emphasize to students that the lesson and activities concentrate on the letter greeting, body, and closing to show the importance of formatting. You may have students add a date and address at the top of each activity if desired.

RULE: In a letter, capitalize the greeting and only the first word of the closing. Use a comma after the greeting and after the closing. Make sure all parts work together to make sense. Separate run-on meanings with capitals and punctuation.

T: "It is important to follow a standard format when writing notes and letters. The 'Letters Have It' section of *Run-on Riddlers* will help show why. Here, you will see very short letters (or notes), often single sentences. They show how the same words can have a different

meaning if not correctly formatted as a letter. Here's an example:"

Show on the board or overhead:
dear sara jane is your best buddy in school abbey

T: "We can tell there are some capitals and punctuation missing. Do we know how to correct it yet?"

S: "It might be a statement *to* Abbey about one person, dear Sara Jane."

T: [Show :]
Dear Sara Jane is your best buddy in school, Abbey.

T: "What if Abbey is telling something?"

S: "Then it's a letter because Abbey wouldn't say her own name."

T: "What should we do with the words?"

S: [Composite of students' suggestions:] The greeting goes on a line by itself. Sara and Jane must be two different people. It's *Dear Sara,* with capitals. The body must have a capital and period. We can add something like *Yours truly,* at the right on its own line and with a comma before the name. The name goes on the last line at right and is capitalized.

T: [Show:]
Dear Sara,
   Jane is your best buddy in school.
         Yours truly,
         Abbey
Is there any way the letter could be a question about Abbey?

S: It would have to be a letter to Dear Sara Jane.

T: [Show:]
Dear Sara Jane,
   Is your best buddy in school?
         Yours truly,
         Abbey

T: "You've seen that there can be several ways to interpret the original words. Keep this in mind as you read directions and do activities in the 'Letters Have It' section of *Run-on Riddlers.*"

Interjections (pp. 24–25)

RULE: Set off an interjection as a separate exclamation. *I like eating. Hey! That's mine.* Some common interjections are *Rats! Darn! Shoot! Wow! Hey! Oh!* Discuss the definition of an interjection:

T: "An interjection stands by itself to show emotion or simple exclamation. It is not a part of any sentence. It is punctuated with an exclamation mark. In the 'Interjections' section, you will find that the interjections have been run on with other thoughts. You must punctuate all sentences and the interjection correctly. An interjection may seem to make sense as part of a sentence. However, you can use the context clues as a guide to help you find the interjections."

Show the following text and discuss the meaning.

We love kittens, so Kate just gave us two rats we forgot to get their collars.

T: "Here is an example that is missing some punctuation. What is the first sentence?"

S: "*We love kittens, so Kate just gave us two*" OR
"*We love kittens, so Kate just gave us two rats.*"

T: "If it is kittens you love, does it make sense that Kate would give you rats?"

S: "No."

T: "So what do you think the word *rats* is used for?"

S: "Since she forgot something, it's probably an interjection."

T: "Where should we add punctuation and capitals?"

S: "Put a period before *rats.*"
"Capitalize *rats.*"
"Put an exclamation mark after *Rats.*"
"Capitalize *We.*"

T: [Show the corrected text.]
We love kittens, so Kate just gave us two. Rats! We forgot to get their collars.
"Remember to look for clues in the context to help you recognize interjections."

Assign 'Interjections' activities.

Quotations (p. 26)

RULE: Enclose spoken words in quotation marks.

T: "For these next activities, you must look carefully to see which words are enclosed in quotation marks. The quotation marks show which words are spoken out loud. The other words are used to help describe the speaker or tell more about what is going on."

Show this text where all can see.

"Listen to that girl," Jon said, "with the voice of an angel."

T: "Who can tell me who had the voice of an angel? Did Jon have the voice of an angel when he spoke?"

S: "No."

T: "Who did have the voice of an angel, and how can you tell?"

S: "The girl had the voice of an angel. You can tell because those words were also inside the quotations."

T: "Yes, the quotations are used only around the words that are spoken. Because they are in quotation marks, we know that Jon said all of these words: *'Listen to that girl with the voice of an angel.'*"

Erase the second set of quotations and the comma to show this:

"Listen to that girl," Jon said with the voice of an angel.
"Now who has the voice of an angel?"

S: "Jon!"

T: "Right. *The voice of an angel* are words used to describe how Jon said something. Keep this in mind as you complete the 'Quotations' activities."

Back and Forth Challenge (pp. 27–29)

Prepare an overhead transparency, or write these on the board:

The mouse ran
The mouse ran in the maze
The mouse ran in the maze were other animals
The mouse ran in the maze were other animals lost

T: "As the sentences build in this section, phrases may go back and forth in position. The same words may go at the end of a sentence at first and then at the beginning of a sentence the next time. Correct each with capitals and ending punctuation. Here's an example, starting with a simple sentence (show the first line):
The mouse ran

T: "This is a sentence, so we put a period at the end." [Do so then show line two.]
The mouse ran in the maze

T: "If we keep the period after *ran*, will we have complete sentences?"

S: "No. We have to put the period after *maze*."

T: "Right." [Put a period after *maze*.]
"Now look at the next version."
The mouse ran in the maze were other animals
"Can we still leave the period after *maze*?

S: "No!"

S: "Yes. *Were other animals* could be a question."

T: "*Were other animals what*? If it said, *The mouse was running in the maze. Were other animals?* that might make a more sensible question. In this case, though, does the wording make it a clear question?"

S: "No. You have to move the period."

T: "Okay." [Show correct punctuation as below.]
The mouse ran. In the maze were other animals.

T: "Now look at the last version."
The mouse ran in the maze were other animals lost

Continue the discussion until students come up with this:

The mouse ran in the maze. Were other animals lost?
[You might also want to point out a second possibility, requiring a comma after the introductory prepositional phrase:]
The mouse ran. In the maze, were other animals lost?

T: "Use these ideas to punctuate and capitalize the sentences in the 'Back and Forth Challenge' activities."

Picture This: Creative Writing Challenge (pp. 30–31)

You may make this section as simple or as challenging as your students need. For example, you may just have them write simple descriptions of the pictures. OR you may want them to design examples of run-on sentences that use the picture as a decoy showing the wrong meaning. They may draw a second picture to show the correct meaning and have a partner pick the correct picture and punctuate the run-on correctly. Note that this can be very challenging and thought provoking. If your students are up to this challenge, and you want to give specific pointers, use the first activity picture and proceed as follows.

T: "This section is a fun way to keep a sharp eye out for run-on meanings. You will write your own sentences to describe a picture you see.
"Look at the first picture on your activity page. How could it show a wrong meaning? What words could be run together to make someone think of this picture? First tell me what is unusual here."

S: "Someone's legs are over their head!"

T: "Yes. Let's start with the words *her legs over her head*." [Show the words as you build the sentences.]
"Since *her legs* are the things that don't usually go with *over her head*, let's separate those ideas."

her legs. Over her head
"We'll add other words to make two sentences. What could be added to the first?"

S: "She stood on, She walked on, etc."

T: "Okay, let's try this."
She moved her legs. Over her head
"Now how can we end the second sentence?"

S: Possible responses:
"was a hanging lamp,"
"she saw the ceiling," etc.

T: *"She moved her legs. Over her head was a hanging lamp.* Those make sense. Now let's take out the period and capital so a partner has to decide how to fix it."
She moved her legs over her head was a hanging lamp.

You may wish to have students draw a picture to show the correct meaning, e.g., showing someone standing up and a lamp over her head. A partner can be asked to pick the correct picture and correct the text with a period and capital as needed. If students write sentences that can make sense written several ways, encourage them to add context clues to limit possible meanings to one.

Picture This: Creative Illustration Challenge (pp. 32–33)

T: "You may have fun with this section by drawing what the text seems to mean before it's corrected and also after it is corrected. Here is an example."
The cat stretches the fish swims in his bowl and hides.
"What meanings can you think of?"

S: "The cat is stretching a fish!"

S: "Or, the cat is stretching and the fish is swimming."

T: "What could you draw to show these meanings?"

Have one or two volunteers draw simple pictures on the board, encouraging, if necessary, until someone draws 1) a cat stretching a fish and 2) a cat stretching itself while a fish swims.

T: "When you finish a page of pictures, trade with your partner and correct the text."

Bobisdrinking
Under the faucet is his cup

ANSWERS

Warmup: Before and After (pp. 1–2)

1. She looked like a <u>monkey</u> business is sneaky.
   She looked like a monkey.
   Monkey business is sneaky.
2. London Bridge is <u>falling down</u> hurts your knees.
   London Bridge is falling down.
   Falling down hurts your knees.
3. Peter Piper led <u>the children</u> followed him like rats.
   Peter Piper led the children.
   The children followed him like rats.
4. I'll love you <u>forever</u> has more days than I can count.
   I'll love you forever.
   Forever has more days than I can count.
5. Spaghetti is <u>slippery food</u> makes you slide on the floor.
   Spaghetti is slippery food.
   Slippery food makes you slide on the floor.
   (Also acceptable: only <u>slippery</u> or <u>food</u>)
6. The Great Squash rises from <u>the garden</u> party was fun.
   The Great Squash rises from the garden.
   The garden party was fun.
7. Don't sit on <u>a porcupine</u> has very sharp quills!
   Don't sit on a porcupine.
   A porcupine has very sharp quills!
8. He rode his <u>skateboard</u> parks are becoming popular.
   He rode his skateboard.
   Skateboard parks are becoming popular.
9. You barked up <u>the wrong tree</u> is never the right tree.
   You barked up the wrong tree.
   The wrong tree is never the right tree.

Over Easy (pp. 3–13)

NOTE: Answers are shown already

corrected (without the editing marks).

1. We must make two complete sentences.
   I ate the hotcakes. Were all of them yours?
2. The dark monsters are large.
   They are small. Dark monsters frighten them.
3. There are two possibilities:
   They drive fast. Cars zoom down the road.
   They drive. Fast cars zoom down the road.
4. There are three sentences each.
   a) **We're out on the jungle gym. Help us. We are falling.** (Also acceptable: *us!* and *falling!*)
   b) **We're out in the jungle. Jim will help us. He can reach high.**
5. The cat cannot be rolling the ball. *Bounces* is not a complete sentence.
   The cat rolls. The ball bounces. The mouse runs away.
6. We can't *Let him in the dryer,* since it leaves a partial sentence (*needs fixing*).
   The repairman is at the door. Let him in. The dryer needs fixing.
7. *String* must be a command.
   Tie your shoe. String those beads. We will be ready to go.
8. *Hot sun* must go with the first sentence, so the sun cannot be moving him.
   She felt the hot sun. Was moving the snowman going to save him?
9. Sentence 2 in *b* can be only a question.
   a) **We shouldn't run. The red light is blinking.**
   b) **We shouldn't run the red light. Is it blinking?**
10. Separate *b* only.
    a) **I will go when he wants me.**
    b) **I will go. When does he want me?**
11. The words *her hair isn't straight* can't be one of the sentences because the words that follow would not make a sentence.

She irons her hair. Isn't straight hair in style?

12. Separate the words *in* and *the*.
 He walked in. The door to the house of mirrors slammed shut.

13. *Dark* is needed to complete the first sentence.
 She stumbled around in the dark. Morning would be brighter.

14. The giraffe must be wearing the glasses. *Makes it easy…* doesn't work.
 Bob has trouble seeing the giraffe. Wearing those glasses makes it easy for the giraffe to see Bob, though!

15. Separate *a* only.
 a) **I always drive. In the house is where I find my keys.**
 b) **He always drives in the house with his toy truck.**

16. Separate as shown.
 a) **The children run into the tree. See the squirrels jump.** (Also acceptable: *jump!*)
 b) **The children run. Into the tree go the squirrels.** (Also acceptable: *squirrels!*)

17. *We are French fried* is wrong because of *we have never been fried*.
 They speak Spanish. Rice is their choice for dinner. They don't like Spanish rice, though.
 We are French. Fried potatoes are our favorite food. We are from France, and we have never been fried.

18. The first *Board* is needed as a verb.
 You lost your skate. Board the plane without it.
 You lost your skateboard. The plane will leave any minute.

19. *Made it easy* would not be a sentence.
 She swatted the fly. Having two-foot arms made it easy.

20. The picture shows the dogs as white.
 The ice cream was white and black. Dogs lapped it up.

21. *Rain* would not be dry.

The ground is hard and dry. Rain soaks into it.

22. *Foot* and *ball* are not a *football*.
 Watch your foot. Ball playing is fun if you're careful.
 Watch your football. Playing is fun, but you might lose your ball.

23. *Go their hats* would make no sense.
 They are ready to celebrate. Up in the air go their hats.
 We are ready to celebrate up in the air. Get in the balloon. (Also acceptable: **… ready. To celebrate up in the air, get in the balloon.**
 However, this requires a comma after an introductory prepositional phrase.)

24. *…a sandwich whole* is wrong because we know *he can't eat it all at once*.
 He can't eat it all at once, but he can eat a sandwich. Whole sandwiches must be cut into tiny pieces for him.

25. *Up the family* would make no sense.
 The sign says there is a drawing for a free vacation. We think we'll need that. Sign up the family.

26. Our teammates wouldn't sit on the bench if *all* the teammates play.
 I know you want to play, but we already picked our teammates. Sit on the bench and watch all the teammates play.

27. Another possibility is *The flowers lie in the field…*, but it cannot be *all. The* because it is unlikely they do that so you can see them up close. It also cannot be *field. So* because the second sentence would be incomplete.
 We saw all the flowers. Lie in the field so you can see them up close.

28. The picture shows the unusual snake.
 The reptile slithered as the man was walking the snake. Wasn't that unusual?

29. Separate only *speed* and *traps*.
 Don't drive at a high speed. Traps are bound to catch you.

30. *The picture orange* is not a sentence.

That's my favorite. Color the picture orange.

31. The soup wasn't warm.

The soup was good cold. Children ate it. They were too hot to eat it warm.

32. A shirt can't cook.

Josh couldn't do his sewing project. I made his shirt. Cook my dinner, and I'll make yours.

Running Picks: Multiple Choice (pp. 14–16)

1. **a** (She doesn't walk in the sky.)
2. **b** (She wouldn't keep clean by wrestling pigs!)
3. **a** (*b* would be an unclear way of saying he was on his way at the moment he became late.)
4. **b** (*gently* and *rough manner* don't go together)
5. **c** (only *c* has complete sentences)
6. **c** (*sofa* wouldn't have a lively bounce; one couldn't *sprawl* with a bounce)
7. **a** (only *a* is sensible and complete)

Running Edits (pp. 17–18)

1. Something was od**d a**bout the new teacher. Mr. Sol was at the front of the roo**m w**hen Hal looked down at his math book. When Hal looked up again, Mr. Sol had disappeare**d. A** cough told Hal that Mr. Sol was now looking over Hal's shoulder.

2. I trained my do**g t**o cook my breakfast. ~~and~~ **H**e's pretty **good at** mixing pancake batte**r.** ~~and~~ **H**e can even pour it on the griddl**e. He** has trouble, though, when it comes to flipping the pancake**s. On** his nose is where they land!

3. We watched the farm animals get smaller and smalle**r. F**loating over the countryside in a hot air balloo**n w**as fun. Dad turned on the burners to keep the air warm in the balloo**n.** ~~and~~ **T**he reason the balloon can float above the land is that hot air is lighter than cool air.

4. Her friend had a comfortable home. Yolanda wondere**d w**hat that would be like. Living in a real hous**e sh**ould be a lot easier than living in her hut. The little shac**k w**as simple and small and had no electricit**y.** ~~and~~ **I**t was a good thing she had a cell phone and a laptop computer.

5. Chocolate is made from the beans of the cacao tre**e.** ~~and~~ **E**ach of its seed pod**s c**an produce about 50 of these white beans. They are drie**d i**n the su**n.** They are taken indoors and packe**d.** ~~and~~ **F**inally, they are sent to the candy makers.

6. I saw a woman getting a tatto**o o**n her arm. The artist put the color in her ski**n by** giving her little shots of ink. The woman said getting the tattoo hurt like bees stingin**g. H**er arm was pretty, but the tattoo would never come of**f.** ~~and~~ **W**ould I ever get a real tattoo**?** I would rather get one of those stick-on tattoos!

Letters Have It (pp. 19–23)

1. **Dear Manuel,**

    Has my bat arrived?

2. a) **1. Dear Aunt Gigi and Uncle Tony have a wonderful time on their vacation.**

    b) **2. Dear Aunt Gigi and Uncle Tony,**

    Have a wonderful time on your vacation!

3. a) **I know you feel guilty about our losing the games. You think the fault is yours, but it is not always yours, Tina.**

    b) **Dear Reggie,**

    I know you feel guilty about our losing the games. You think the fault is yours, but it is not.

    Yours always,
    Tina

4. **Dear Uncle,**

    Janine said you would not like the exchange student, but I know you will.

    Love,
    Bjorn

5. a) **Dear Billy Jo has a gift for you. He pretends it isn't for you, but I know it is yours truly, Jaime.**
b) **Dear Billy,**
> **Jo has a gift for you. He pretends it isn't for you, but I know it is.**
> > > **Yours truly,**
> > > **Jaime**

Interjections (pp. 24–25)

1. *It* shows that *pet* doesn't go with *rats*. The dog must be her pet.
> **I really liked her new pet. Rats! It just ran away.**

2. *Darn* makes sense only as an interjection (you don't fix a wall by darning).
> **My great granny will not help me. Darn! I was hoping she would fix the hole in my wall.**

3. *Oh* is not the missing letter.
> **I am missing the letter. Oh! Here it is. It is the letter em.**

4. The arrangements below meet the requirements given.
> a) **He's going for target practice with a bow and arrow. He wants me to go shoot. I'd rather play soccer.**
> b) **He's going for target practice with a bow and arrow. He wants me to go. Shoot! I'd rather play soccer.**

5. *Hay* is food for horses. *Hey* is not.
> **The horses get mean if they don't eat hay. Give them that bale!**
> **The horses get mean if they don't eat. Hey! Give them that bale!**

Quotations (p. 26)

1. **Mom** has the spoon

2. When not in quotation marks, *very loudly* describes the speaker.
> Ronik speaks loudly. **a**
> Ronik wants John to play loudly. **b**

3. Used in the quotation, *eyes wide open* refers to the fish and not to the speaker.
> "Do we get to eat that fish?" he asked with eyes wide open. **b**

"Do we have to eat that fish," he asked, "with eyes wide open?" **a**

Back & Forth Challenge (pp. 27–29)

1. **He took a bath in the tub.**
He took a bath. In the tub were lots of bubbles.
He took a bath in the tub. Were lots of bubbles popping in his face?
He took a bath. In the tub were lots of bubbles popping in his face.

2. **The spaceships flew.**
The spaceships flew around the planet.
The spaceships flew. Around the planet was a belt of asteroids.
The spaceships flew around the planet. Was a belt of asteroids acting as a shield?
The spaceships flew. Around the planet was a belt of asteroids acting as a shield.
(Also acceptable: Constructions that include a prepositional phrase: Around the planet, was…?)

3. **She picked an apple.**
She picked an apple from the tree.
She picked an apple. From the tree fell two.
She picked an apple. From the tree fell two birds.
She picked an apple. From the tree fell two. Birds fly away.
She picked an apple. From the tree fell two birds. Fly away.

4. **A baseball was found.**
A baseball was found under the window.
A baseball was found. Under the window were pieces of glass.
A baseball was found under the window. Were pieces of glass?
A baseball was found. Under the window were pieces of glass that fell when it crashed.
(Also acceptable: 1) A baseball was found under the window. Were pieces of glass that fell when it crashed?

Constructions that include a prepositional phrase: Under the window, were...?)

5. **He loved to travel.**
   He loved to travel in Mexico.
   He loved to travel. In Mexico were his sisters.
   He loved to travel in Mexico. Were his sisters working?
   He loved to travel in Mexico. Were his sisters working on the family business?
   He loved to travel. In Mexico were his sisters working on the family business.
   He loved to travel. In Mexico were his sisters. Working on the family business was fun.
   He loved to travel in Mexico. Were his sisters working on the family? Business was fun.

[Also acceptable: Constructions that include a prepositional phrase: In Mexico, were...?]

Picture This: Creative Writing Challenge (pp. 30–31)

Answers will vary.
Evaluation criteria:
The student
  1a) writes a complete sentence of his own that illustrates the picture.
  2a) identifies and communicates, in rough form, two possible meanings related to the picture(s).
  3a) writes text that includes ambiguity and clue(s) for a partner to correct.
  Also: Given partner's paper, chooses the correct meaning for the picture.

Picture This: Creative Illustration Challenge (pp. 32–33)

Answers will vary.
Evaluation criteria:
The student
  1a) draws a picture that illustrates the intended meaning of the sentence.
  2a) draws an additional picture, illustrating the run-on (incorrect) meaning for a partner.
  Also: Given partner's paper,
  1b) corrects the text to make complete sentences.
  2b) identifies relationship of text to partner's drawings (matches pictures to meanings and/or identifies whether picture matches text meaning).